So Many Warm Words

Selections from the Poetry of Rosa Nevadovska

A bilingual edition of Yiddish poems

translated by
Merle L. Bachman

Teaneck, New Jersey

So Many Warm Words, English translation ©2024 Merle Bachman. All rights reserved. No part of this book may be used or reproduced in any manner whatsoever without written permission except in the case of brief quotations embodied in critical articles and reviews.

Published by Ben Yehuda Press
122 Ayers Court #1B
Teaneck, NJ 07666

http://www.BenYehudaPress.com

To subscribe to our monthly book club and support independent Jewish publishing, visit https://www.patreon.com/BenYehudaPress

Jewish Poetry Project #36 http://jpoetry.us

Ben Yehuda Press books may be purchased at a discount by synagogues, book clubs, and other institutions buying in bulk. For information, please email markets@BenYehudaPress.com

Cover photo courtesy Alice Saitzeff Grossman.

The Yiddish poems in this volume originally appeared in *Azoy vi ikh bin* (Los Angeles: Rosa Nevadovska Literary Committee, 1936) and *Lider mayne* (Ed. Avrom Lis. Tel Aviv: I. L. Peretz, 1974).

ISBN13 978-1-963475-26-5 pb 978-1-963475-27-2 epub

Library of Congress Cataloging-in-Publication Data

24 25 26 / 10 9 8 7 6 5 4 3 2 1   20240722

Contents

Acknowledgements	vii
Introduction	ix
Overturned	2
In a Field	4
At the Crossing of Noisy Streets	6
*	8
Today	10
Sweatshop	12
Dusk	14
The Girl Who Operates the Elevator	16
A Home in the Bronx	18
On East Broadway	20
Because You Were Not Here	22
*	24
Park and Wind	26
Four in the Morning	28
At Night	30
*	32
A Poem Like That	34
*	36
So Many Warm Words	38
Letters	40
*	42
Images	44
Silence	46
Mother's Death	48
Like a Bee	50
*	52
A Little Poem	54

War	56
At My Window	58
Tree in a Field	60
Butterflies	62
A Mountain of Pain	64
Snow	66
On the Final Road	68
Pay Attention	70
For Darling Leah	72
Going to Sleep	74
Mother and Child	76
Fire-Script	78
A Vision	80
*	82
At the Shore	84
Yearning	86
Morning-joy	88
Desert	90
Seen	92
Sea	94
Obedient	96
I Have Seen	98
About the Author	101
About the Translator	101

Acknowledgements

I am deeply grateful to Yiddish scholars and translators Kathryn Hellerstein, Sheva Zucker, and Faith Jones, for their help and guidance over the years as I worked on the translations in this volume. Special thanks to the Yiddish Book Center for granting me a Translation Fellowship in 2015-16, for which I produced a draft of this book, and especially to Book Center staff Sebastian Schulman and Madeleine (Mindl) Cohen, for their interest and support.

Above all, I acknowledge with deep appreciation and gratitude the wonderful Alice Saitzeff Grossman, literary heir to the works of Rosa Nevadovska (her "Aunt Rose"), for permission to use the selected Yiddish texts herein and to publish my translations.

I am very grateful to the editors of the following journals for publishing earlier versions of poems in this anthology, as follows:

"I Have Seen" in *Pakn Treger*, Yiddish Book Center, Spring 2017 (online).
"In a Field" and "A Home in the Bronx" in the *Blue Lyra Review*, 2017 (online).
"Mother and Child" and "On the Final Road" (in my article, "Reflections on Yiddish Poetry and War"), in *Paideuma*, Volume 47, 2020.
"Dusk," "So Many Words," "Like a Bee," and "Yearning" in *The Louisville Review*, Summer 2023.

Introduction

Rosa Nevadovska: Her photographic portrait is solemn, searching. Her eyes look past the photographer — past us, as we look at her.

She lived an unsettled and at times a lonely life, as many of her poems suggest. Her poems also reveal a life that was rich, complex, attuned to what can only be heard in silence, and filled with scattered moments of sheer joy.

Nevadovska's biography, in brief, is as follows[1]:

Zelda Reyzl (Rosa) was born in 1890, the eldest of seven children, into a traditional yet worldly Jewish family in Bialystok where she was schooled in both Jewish and Russian subjects. Her first publications were in Russian and appeared in two Russian newspapers published in her home city. From the map of her wandering afterwards, one gets the sense that Bialystok simply could not contain or satisfy someone of her intellectual hunger, for she continued her studies in Ghent and Brussels; at the Russian Free Academy in Berlin; and briefly at the Sorbonne in Paris, where the poet worked in the lab of Marie Curie. At the age of 23, Nevadovksa married a man named Yisroel Kessel. The marriage ended rapidly in divorce, and Nevadovska gave birth to a daughter, Leah. During a bitterly cold winter in Moscow, where the poet stayed during World World I, she lost her daughter to meningitis (1915). Leah was two years old.

Immediately after the war, the poet continued her solo travels: first, home to Bialystok, then on to Berlin. She did not move to America until 1928, when she was 38 years old — and here, her restlessness resumed. First, she lived in New York City, then in Los Angeles, then back to Brooklyn and the Bronx. She also traveled often, giving lectures and sometimes teaching, and publishing

---

[1] The brief biography here is based on information available in the *Naye leksikon fun der Yidisher literatur* (New Lexicon of Yiddish Literature). Ed. Efroyim Oyerbukh, Ya'akov Birnboym, Eliahu Shulman and Moyshe Shtarkman. Volume 6. (New York: World Jewish Congress, 1965). In addition, I drew on the biographical sketch provided by "S. K." (Sima Kaplan, one of Nevadovska's sisters who had emigrated to the U.S. in 1921) in *Lider mayne*.

her poetry in a variety of Yiddish newspapers and journals. It was in Los Angeles in 1936 that she published her single collection of poetry, *Azoy vi ikh bin* (As I Am). Despite love affairs hinted at in her poetry, Nevadovska lived alone for most of her life.

"Home" is not a word that appears in more than a handful of Nevadovska's poems, and then, only in connection with Bialystok, her parents and the world she'd left behind. In addition to poems engaging, often painfully, with Old Country memories, one finds poems relating poignantly with the American cityscape around her. More significantly (at least to me), are the poems involving an interior world, sensed late at night or in the spaces of contemplation in which silence itself speaks. Her own poetry becomes a recurring subject: in some poems it is her *basherter*, her fated love; in others, it seems to constitute her in body and in spirit. Although even a limited look at Nevadovska's correspondence reveals that she had a rich circle of literary colleagues and friends in Los Angeles and in New York, it seems as if she was most befriended by poetry itself. It is poetry that gave her life meaning and, in a sense, watched over her.

I have chosen to translate only three poems from *Azoy vi ikh bin*, because the poems it includes strike me as less developed than her later work, as well as limited by their historical timeframe (e.g., there are poems celebrating the red flags of the Soviet revolution, the first of May, and "brothers" working the land in the Soviet Jewish Autonomous Region, i.e., Birobidzhan). In contrast, the poems that were collected in the anthology *Lider mayne* (My Poetry), published after Nevadovska passed away in 1971, reflect deeper life experience and greater poetic sophistication. It is from this posthumous book that I have drawn the bulk of poems found translated here.[2]

Lider mayne, which contains about 250 pages of poetry, was published in 1974 in Tel Aviv by the well-respected press, Peretz Farlag. The anthology resulted from the collaboration of two of Nevadovska's better-known and esteemed colleagues: the poet,

---

[2] The poems I chose to translate from *Azoy vi ikh bin* are "*A meydl firt dem elevator*" (p. 17, herein), "*A barg payn*" (p. 65) and "*In letstn gang*" (p. 69) and appear in a different Yiddish font.

Binem Heller, who edited and arranged the text, and the literary critic Avrom Lis, who introduced the book with his short essay, *Vegn der dikhterin* (About the poet) *Roza Nevadovska*. In his introduction, Lis points out that the Yiddish word *benkshaft* — meaning longing, or yearning, or nostalgia — surfaces often in Nevadovska's poems. This makes sense to me. Like many Eastern European Jews of her generation, and especially as an immigrant to the U.S. before World War II, Nevadovska had unknowingly said goodbye forever to family members and friends, and the terrible losses she suffered led to her being shadowed by depression and regret. The poems in *Lider mayne* address the devastation of the Holocaust; they also crystallize the poet's personal suffering and her moments of hope and gratitude to God.

The poems gathered here, in *So Many Warm Words*, are a small selection from *Lider mayne* that vary in subject yet share some common attributes: they are, overall, quiet, empathic, meditative, and poignant. In emotional tone they move from loneliness and loss to pure, joyous moments of transcendence. Examples of the latter include poems from Nevadovska's years in California, set at the Pacific shore or high in the Sierras. While many Yiddish poets have written of American natural landscapes, I have yet to find other poems like these, which express a mystical sense of spiritual connection to nature.

Further, most of the poems I chose to translate were written in highly compressed forms, which set off their vivid images and emotions. In the original Yiddish, many consist of just two rhymed quatrains, in meters varying from iambic tetrameter to iambic pentameter. Sometimes Nevadovska's poetic strategy reminds me of Emily Dickinson's, in that the poems' tight structures are often subverted by their content. Rarely could I transfer the rhyming intact to my English versions — however, I've been careful to include sound echoes within and among stanzas, that suggest rhyme without reproducing it. I've also been attentive to keeping the length and rhythm of the poems' lines wherever I could. If you can read Yiddish, you will enjoy reading the originals of the translations, on facing pages in this volume.

The poems in *Lider mayne* were never published in newspapers or journals while Nevadovska lived, and it was her request to her family that they be published upon her death. I consider them to be a treasure trove from which I have plucked some special jewels, "so many warm words" despite the passage of time and the necessity of translation to make them available to you, here and now.

—Merle Bachman

So Many Warm Words

Overturned

A black hand has leafed through a newspaper,
A red rooster crowed forth its tidings.
And I remain suspended in the night
In joy and sadness, half-awake, half-asleep.

An anxious blue diffuses everywhere.
From the abyss, a ship slowly rises.

All sounds are halted, muted.
Mountains topple over in the deep.

Rosa Nevadovska

איבערגעקערט

א שװארצע האנט האט דורכגעמישט א בלאט,‏
א רויטער האן — א בשורה אויסגעקרייט.‏
געזען, געהערט — געבליבן אין דער נאכט
איך בין האלב װאך — אין טרויער און אין פרייד.‏

א פחד-בלויקייט שפרייט זיך אויס ארום.‏
פון טיפענישן טויכט ארויס א שיף.‏
די קלאנגען װערן אפגעשטעלט און שטום.‏
די בערג זיך קערן איבער אין דער טיף.‏

In a Field

In a field I saw the dawn emerge.
The sky caught fire, then was quenched.
And someone delivered a message
In obscure, colorful language.

And I myself was like the sky,
Kindling my melody with blue and red.
At sunrise I saw myself come into view:
The blue of my happiness, the red of my wounds.

אין פעלד

אין פעלד האָב איך געזען דעם אויפגיי פונעם טאָג.
דער הימל האָט געצונדן זיך, געלאָשן.
און עמעצער האָט עפּעס אָנגעזאָגט
מיט אומפארשטענדלעך און קאָליריק לשון.

און ווי דער הימל — כ׳בין אליין געווען.
מיט בלוי און רויט מיַן ניגון כ׳האָב געצונדן.
אין אויפגאַנג האָב איך זיך אליין דערזען:
אין בלוי פון גליק, אין רויט פון מיַנע ווונדן.

At the Crossing of Noisy Streets

At the crossing of noisy streets
I waited for you on the corner.
The rattle and roar of automobiles
Cut pieces from my day.

I recalled the snowy heads of mountains,
They spoke to me of loneliness...
It's good for two, together, to take a single road.
And I waited for you until late.

בײַם איבערקרייץ פֿון רוישיקע גאַסן

בײַם איבערקרייץ פֿון רוישיקע גאַסן
האָב איך געוואַרט אויף דיר בײַם ראָג.
מאַשינען האָבן מיט רודער און רעשן
געשניטן שטיקער פֿון מײַן טאָג.

כ'האָב דערמאָנט זיך די בערג־קעפּ אין שנייען,
זיי האָבן וועגן אײנזאַמקייט גערעדט —
אַז גוט איז אײן וועג גיין אין צווייען...
און געוואַרט אויף דיר האָב איך ביז שפּעט.

*

The dusk is copper-red and rose;
Every window reflects its glow.
In a field, the grass deepens its green
And the dust falls still on the road.

Here, the city's clamor just gets louder
As masses of tired people head home.
The evening casts itself in gray steel
And in the crowds — each person is alone.

✡

דער פֿאַרנאַכט איז קופּעררויט און רױז
און זײַן גלאַנץ שפּיגלט זיך אין יעדער שױב.
גרינער װערט אין פֿעלד דאָס גראָז,
און שטילער אױפֿן װעג — דער שטױב.

נאָר שטאָט װערט רוישיקער װי אַלע מאָל,
די מענטשן ציִען מידע זיך אַהיים.
דער אָװנט גיסט זיך דאָ װי גרויער שטאָל,
און אין דער ענגשאַפֿט — יעדער בלײַבט אַלײן.

Today

I wander up and down the streets. Distant people feel close:
I carry your words with me, from your poem — its slender flame.
My heart is open. Today, in silence, I want to bless —
Earth, waters, forests — along with you and me.

הײַנט

איך גיי גאס-אײַן, גאס-אויס. ס'ווערן נאענט מיר ווײַטע מענטשן :

איך טראג דײַן ווארט מיט זיך, פֿון דײַן ליד — דעם דינעם פֿלאם.

מײַן הארץ איז אפֿן. מיט ליפן שטומע ווילט זיך מיר הײַנט בענטשן —

די ערד, די וואסערן, די וועלדער — מיט זיך און מיט דיר צוזאם.

So Many Warm Words

Sweatshop

So Leah traveled back from the shop,
Leah rode homeward, rode home.
The pines broke into a prayerful sway,
And her heart uttered a bitter moan.

The days were on the cusp of spring
With pure mornings, frozen dew.
How the girl yearned, longed without end
For forest and field, for sky's blue.

Then Leah traveled again to the shop,
To sew clothes — sew up the days.
The subway still pounded inside her head,
While her longing beat out its own way.

So Leah went into the dimly lit shop,
Cheeks stained, and lips painted, red.
Her own youthful blush she had already stitched
Into clothing for strangers, instead.

Rosa Nevadovska

שאַפּ

איז לאה געפאָרן פון שאַפּ צוריק,
איז לאה געפאָרן אַהיים, אַהיים,
האָבן זיך פּלוצעם די סאָסנעם צעוויגט,
דאָס האַרץ האָט געיאָמערט אַ ביטער געוויין.

געווען ערב־פרילינגדיק זײַנען די טעג
מיט לויטערע מאָרגנס, געפרוירענעם טוי.
געבענקט האָט דאָס מיידל, געבענקט אָן אַ ברעג,
נאָך וואַלד און נאָך פעלד, נאָך דעם הימלישן בלוי.

איז לאה געפאָרן ווידער אין שאַפּ,
קליידער צו נייען — פאַרנייען די טעג.
די סאָבווי אין קאַפּ — אַ קלאַפּ נאָך אַ קלאַפּ,
און ס׳קלאַפּט אויס די בענקשאַפט איר אייגענעם שטעג.

איז לאה געקומען אין פינצטערן שאַפּ,
די באַקן געפאַרבטע, די ליפּן, אויף רויט.
איר רויטקייט די יונגע, פון אייגענער באַק,
האָט לאה אין קליידער די פרעמדע פאַרנייט.

So Many Warm Words

Dusk

I saw the sun through wintery trees,
Through the lattice of naked black boughs.
Violet colors spoke to me of depths
And stillness in a secret tongue.

I walked through the quiet winter gardens.
Minutes earlier, the sun had set.
I thought of you and blue, far-off places and all
Around me I saw signs, clues.

The sun had gone, leaving only gray;
The west was dark, all colors subdued.
And that moment brought to me your face,
From distant years — your eyes, and your language.

פאר נאכט

איך האב געזען די זון דורך ווינטערדיקע ביימער,
דורך דעם געפלעכט פון הוילע שוואַרצע צווייַגן.
די פיאלעט-פארבן האבן אויף א שפראך געהיימער
גערעדט צו מיר די שפראך פון טיפעניש און שווייַגן.

איך בין געגאנגען דורך די שטילע ווינטערדיקע גערטנער.
די זון האט זיך געזעצט שוין אין די לעצטע רגעם.
געטראכט האב איך פון דיר און פון די בלויע ערטער,
און אלץ האט אויסגעזען בלויז ווי אן אנדייַט און א רמז.

פארגאנגען איז די זון, און אלץ ארום איז גרוי געווארן,
דער מערב האט געטונקלט און די פארבן אויסגעלאשן.
און יענע רגע האט געבראכט צו מיר פון ווייַטע יארן
דייַן פנים, דייַנע אויגן און דייַן לשון.

The Girl Who Operates the Elevator

Day never penetrates this place.
An eternal dusk reigns,
Whether the door is open or the door is closed.

The route goes up and down,
A pail pulled from a well...
Full of people who trickle away like water.
At different floors, they come, they go.

The girl who operates the machine...
I cannot forget her painfully
thin limbs.

When I roam the noisy streets,
She follows me. And the elevator's darkness
Has become part of her.

I see her colorless face, her sunken cheeks...
Like wax, daubed red with cheap powder.
Her silenced mouth still cries to me,

Out of shadowed days in the elevator's nook.
Her slender hands, pale fingers with painted nails,
Extend like wasted branches on a tree...

Her gloomy eyes reflect the light of a little bulb
That burns all day over her head
Like a Yahrzeit candle.

אַ מײדל פֿירט דעם עלעוװײטאָר

דער טאָג דרינגט אַהין קײנמאָל נישט אַרײן...
דאָרט הערשט אַן אײביק פֿאַרנאַכט,
צו ס'איז אָפֿן די טיר, צו די טיר איז פֿאַרמאַכט.

אַרױף און אַראָפּ איז דער װעג,
װי פֿון אַן עמער אין ברונעם...
פֿול מיט מענטשן, װעלכע צערינען, װי װאַסער—
אין פֿאַרשײדענע עטאַזשן, זײ גײען, זײ קומען.

די מײדל, װאָס פֿירט די מאַשין...
איך קען נישט פֿאַרגעסן דעם שטילן פֿײן
פֿון אירע דינע, פֿאַרדאַרטע גלידער.

װען איך גײ איבער רױשיקע גאַסן,—
גײט זי מיר נאָך. און דער טונקלער װינקל
פֿון עלעװײטאָר איז װי צוגעװאַקסן צו איר.

איך זע איר פּנים בלאַסן, אירע אײנגעפֿאַלענע באַקן...
זײ זײנען װי װאַקס, באַפֿאַרבטער מיט בליקן רױט.
איר פֿאַרשטילטער מױל שרײַט צו מיר, שרײַט.

שרײַט פֿון פֿאַרטונקלטע טעג אין װינקל פֿון עלעװײטאָר.
אירע דינע הענט, די בלײכע פֿינגער, מיט די באַפֿאַרבטע נעגל,
ציטערן זיך, װי אָפּגעדאַרטע צװײגן אױף אַ יעשנדיקן בױם...

אין אירע אומעטיקע אױגן שפּיגלט-זיך שײן פֿון אַ לעמפּל,
װאָס ברענט דעם גאַנצן טאָג איבער איר קאָפּ,
װי אַ יאָרצײַט-ליכט...

A Home in the Bronx

In these rooms, there is no one — just silence.
It's a home in the exile of memory.
An hour flutters quietly by like a lonely bird —
The years have kept this silence undisturbed.

You call this *home*, but it's foreign,
Not the Jewish city where I was born.
Such a home gives no warmth. Like a borrowed shirt
It was made for someone else.

אַ היים אין די בראָנקס

שטיל איז אין די צימערן, קיינער איז ניטאָ.
ס'איז אַ היים אין פרעמדקייט פון זכרון.
ווי אַ פויגל איינזאַם פּאַכעט שטיל אַ שעה —
שטיל שוין, אַ באַרויִקטע פון יאָרן.

רופסט עס היים, נאָר ס'איז אַ היים אין פרעמד,
ניט די שטאָט די ייִדישע, ווּ כ'בין געבאָרן.
אַזאַ היים — זי וואָרעמט ניט, ווי אַ געבאַרגטע העמד,
וואָס איז פאַר עמעצן גענייט געוואָרן.

On East Broadway

In the air, the voice of Avrom Reyzen lingers.
But I can still hear the echo of his words.
Yet all is dust now, like a rose's shriveled petals,
And all is changed, though the place remains the same.

Right here — just now it seems — we were sitting at his table,
Taking in the goodness of his clever speech, like bread.
Now strangers sit here. They drink and eat,
And get their news from thumbing through the papers.

אויף איסט־בראָדוויי

דאָ שוועבט נאָך אין דער לופט די שטים פון אברהם רייזען,
מיר דוכט זיך, אז איך הער נאָך אַלץ דעם עכאָ פון זײַן וואָרט.
נאָר אַלץ איז איצט צעשטויבט, ווי בלעטעלעך טרוקענע פון
רויזן,
און אַלץ איז אַנדערש, כאָטש דאָס זעלביקע געבליבן איז
דאָס אָרט.

אָט דאָ, נאָר וואָס — מיר דוכט — מיר זײַנען בײַ זײַן טיש
געזעסן,
געשלונגען זײַנע קלוגע גוטע רייד, ווי ברויט, צו זאַט.
איצט זיצן פרעמדע דאָ. זיי טרינקען און זיי עסן,
און גלײַכגילטיק זיי לייענען די נײַעסן פון בלאַט.

1957

Because You Were Not Here

I walked with him, because you were not here.
Everyone I passed reminded me of you.
So I strolled with him, and he glowed, he yearned,
At my hands' slightest touch, he burned.

And he gave quite a speech — he spoke of joy and rest.
I listened not a bit to those sounds of his.
Only you did I seek, only you were my quest —
And among thousands, I was with you alone.

װײַל דו ביסט ניט געװען

איך האָב מיט אים שפּאַצירט, װײַל דו ביסט ניט געװען.
איך האָב אויף יעדן איינעם דײַנם אַן ענלעכקייט געזען.
בין איך מיט אים געגאַנגען. ער האָט געגליט, געברענט
בײַם מינדעסטן באַריר פֿון מײַנע קליינע הענט.

און ריײד האָט ער גערעדט — ריײד פֿון רו און פֿרײד.
איך האָב זיך גאָרניט צוגעהערט צום קלאַנג פֿון זײַנע ריײד.
נאָר דיך האָב איך געזוכט, נאָר דיך האָב איך געזען,
און צװישן טויזנטער — מיט דיר אַליין געװען.

So Many Warm Words

*

How sad and cold the toil
That dresses us for holiday leisure.
Behind your dark eyelashes
Sparks a sunny joy.

Lips open, searching
For the ripe fruit of a kiss.
With spicy and earthy odors
Our breath fills with pleasure.

✡

ווי טרויעריק און קיל די מי איז,
וואס טוט אן אונדז א יומטובדיק קלייד.
דורך דײַנע טונקעלע ווײעם
צעפלאמט זיך א זוניקע פרייד.

די ליפן עפענען זיך, זוכן
ווי א זאפטיקע פרוכט — א קוש.
געווירצטיקע און ערדישע גערוכן
פארפולן אונדזער אטעם מיט גענום.

So Many Warm Words

Park and Wind

The moon now has a three-quarter face
In the quiet, night-time park.
The trees shiver as if in danger,
Withered limbs reach out in the dark.

Wind lulls the trees, the branches
In night's silvery cradle.
Suddenly — all is still. The park slumbers.
Only my unrest stays wakeful.

פּאַרק און ווינט

דרײַ פערטל פון פנים האָט הײַנט די לבנה
אין שטילן, אין נאַכטיקן פּאַרק.
די ביימער פאַרצימטערטע, ווי אין אַ ספנה,
די צווייַגן זיך שטרעקן פאַרדאַרט.

אַ ווינט וויגט דעם פּאַרק — די ביימער, די צווייַגן,
אין זילבערנער וויג פון דער נאַכט.
און פלוצעם ווערט שטיל, און סודותדיק שווייַגן
ווערט שלאָף. בלויז מײַן אומרו ווערט וואַך.

Four in the Morning

The things around me absorb language:
The table launches mutely into speech.
The last stars start to fade
And each minute has a different worth.

Now I too see differently —
Each thing has its own meaning.
People sleep, but the walls keep awake —
Guarding precious time, drop by drop.

פיר פאַר טאָג

די זאַכן מיר אַרום באַקומען לשון:
דער טיש האָט מיט אַ שטומשפּראַך זיך צערעדט.
די לעצטע שטערן װערן אויסגעלאָשן
און יעדע רגע האָט אַן אַנדער װערט.

און אַנדערש אויך דערזע איך איצט די זאַכן —
אַ יעדע מיט אַנדערן באַטײַט.
די מענטשן שלאָפֿן, נאָר די װענט — זײ װאַכן
און היטן גיריק יעדן טראָפּן צײַט.

So Many Warm Words

At Night

At night, life is — another life.
Silence receives a voice, darkness — light.
And all species, web upon web,
Show their true face.

And when shadows rise from corners,
A whole other reality unfurls.
Scraps of light flare up and sparkle,
Heralds from *there* — a secret world.

בײַ נאַכט

בײַ נאַכט דאָס לעבן — איז אַן אַנדער לעבן.
די שטילקייט קריגט אַ שטים, דער חושך — ליכט.
און אַלע מינים ווידמונגען־געוועבן
באַווײַזן זייער אמתדיק געזיכט.

און ווען די שאָטנס שטײַגן פֿון די ווינקלען,
דאַן וויקלט אויף זיך גאָר אַן אַנדער וואָר.
די בערגלעך שײַן צעפֿלעמלען זיך און פֿינקלען —
שטאַפּעטעלעך פֿון סודותדיקן ד אָ ר ט.

So Many Warm Words

*

Where was I, before I came to be?
And where will I be, after having been?
Am I here by accident, a flicker of light,
An eye, where the world reflects itself through my sight?

Who am I? A child at a window, awe-struck?
And what are thoughts — ideas that strike and spark?
What is this around me? The dust of disintegration?
Or something-out-of-nothing — the actual Creation?

וווּ בין איך געוועןן אין מײַן איידער-זײַן?
און ווּ וועל איך זײַן נאָך מײַן האָבן געוועןן?
בין איך בלויז אַ צופאַל, אַ שטראַלעלעכל שײַן,
אַן אויג, ווּ עס שפּיגלט זיך וועלט דורך מײַן זען?

ווער בין איך? אַ קינד אין פאַרגאַפּ בײַ אַ שויב?
און וואָס איז מײַן טראַכטן, דער אויפפלײַכט פון רעיון?
וואָס איז דער אַרום? אַ צעפּאַל אינעם שטויב,
צי גאָר דער באַשאַף פון דעם יש מאין?

So Many Warm Words

A Poem Like That

My poem's lines, red as rubies
Fly across territories, across time.
Will I encounter them again
On my way into the very farthest place?

My poem's lines, blue as sapphires,
Brightly swim between reality and dream.
Gloom and sorrows guide me
From the abyss into the radiance of space.

My poem's lines — stars on high —
All precious stones, color upon color.
Tell me, Creator, will I reach them
Even before I die?

אַ ליד אַזאַ

מײַנע שורות רויטע, ווי רובינען,
פליִען צווישן שטח, צווישן צײַט.
וועל איך ווידער זיי אַ מאָל געפֿינען
אויף מײַן וועג צו סאַמע לעצטער ווײַט?

מײַנע שורות בלויע, ווי סאַפּירן,
שווימען העלע צווישן וואָר און טרוים.
אומעטן און צערן מיך פֿירן
פֿון דעם תּהום ביז ליכטיקייט פֿון רוים.

מײַנע שורות — שטערן אין די הייכן —
אַלע איידלשטיינער, פֿאַרב נאָך פֿאַרב.
זאָג, באַשעפֿער, וועל איך זיי דערגרייכן
איידער נאָך איך שטאַרב?

So Many Warm Words

*

No *thing* is silent.
Everything possesses a voice.
There are no mute objects.
Even steel can clamor awake.
When burned,
It hisses resistance.
It turns pale, then reddens
And when it cools
Becomes a wheel,
Thundering its rebuke
Over the roads.

☆

קיין זאך איז ניט שטום.
אַלץ האָט אַ קול.
ניטאָ קיין שטומע זאכן.
אויך דער שטאַל
קאָן אין ליאַרעם דערוואכן.
ווען מען ברענט אים —
שיפּעט ער אַנטקעגן.
ער ווערט בלאַס, ער ווערט רויט,
און ווען ער קילט זיך אָפּ —
ווערט ער ראָד,
וואָס דונערט
און בייזערט זיך איבער די ווענגן.

So Many Warm Words

So many warm words
Spoken into cold ears.
So many strange places
Humming with their own life.

And long had I gone, so long,
On my own on a bright path,
Filling my lungs with song,
Climbing alone up the stairs.

That warm breath of hope
When I got to the top,
Exhaled on a frosty night —
No one awaited me there.

אזוי פיל וואַרעמע ווערטער

אזוי פיל וואַרעמע ווערטער
אין קאַלטע אויערן גערעדט.
אזוי פיל פרעמדע ערטער
מיט אייגענעם לעבן באַלעבט.

און לאַנג, אזוי לאַנג געגאַנגען
אַליין אויפן ליכטיקן וועג,
מיט אָטעם אין מײַנע געזאַנגען
געשטיגן אַליין אויף די טרעפּ.

דעם וואַרעמען אָטעם פון האָפן
געהויכט אויף אַ פראָסטיקער נאַכט,
און וועמען האָב איך דאָרט געטראָפן?
ס'האָט קיינער אויף מיר ניט געוואַרט.

So Many Warm Words

Letters

A bundle of letters...dust and perfume
From somewhere out of the land of youth.
A bridle from a warrior's proud horse.
A red scalp. A sword's silvery hilt.

A handful of letters...I sit with them and muse
How, in battle, the heart is blind to tears:
When his eyes stared open wide in fear
I took the scalp, turned on my heel and left.

Rosa Nevadovska

בריוו

א פּעקל בריוו... עס שמעקט מיט דופט און שטויב
פון ערגעצלאַנד, פון יוגנטלאַנד אַרויס.
א זילבערצויים פון קריגערס שטאָלצן פערד.
א רויטער סקאַלפּ. א הענטל פון א שוערד.

א בינטל בריוו... איך זיץ בײַ דעם און קלער,
ווי בלינד דאָס האַרץ איז קריגסצייט פאר א טרער:
ווען יענעמס אויג האָט זיך צעגלאַצט אין שרעק,
האָב איך סקאַלפּירט, געכאפט עס און אַוועק.

So Many Warm Words   41

*

On the journeys that take us so far,
Something frightens us, there.
Is it too late for us, or too early?
No one has asked this yet.

After all, what are words? — Hail
On a field that's burst into bloom.
It's good now to wander, to roam
In somebody's world, somewhere.

✡

אין אונדזערע װײטע נסיעות
איז עפּעס פֿאַראַן, װאָס עס שרעקט.
צו שפּעט שוין פֿאַר אונדז, צי צו פֿרי איז?
נאָר קיינער האָט נאָך ניט געפֿרעגט.

װײַל װאָס זײַנען װערטער? — אַ האָגל
אויף אַקערשט צעפּוכעטן פֿעלד.
ס'איז גוט איצט צו זײַן אינעם װאָגל
אין עמעצנס ערגעץ אַ װעלט...

So Many Warm Words

Images

Images of my mother and father, still glimmering —
A light drifts to me from mother's face.
From my father wafts a smell of early spring,
Earth refreshed by dew's frozen trace.

I love every blade of grass — and blue flowers
That wander amid the rye, lost in the field.
But my grandfather's eyes — in them I see sorrow.
In my childish world, darkness is revealed.

געשטאַלטן

געשטאַלטן פֿון טאָטן און מאַמען נאָך פֿליסן —
אַ ליכט צו מיר שװימט פֿון דער מאַמעס געזיכט.
פֿון טאַטן דערטראָגט זיך אַ ריח פֿון ניסן —
פֿון ערד מיט געפֿרױרענעם טױ שױן דערקװיקט.

כ׳האָב ליב יעדעם גרעזל, פֿון בלומען — די בלױע,
װאָס בלאָנדזשען אַרום צװישן קאָרן און פֿעלד.
נאָר זע איך די אױגן פֿון זײדן אין טרױער —
פֿאַרשטעלט װערט מיט חושך מײַן קינדערשע װעלט.

Silence

Red carrots, blue-tinged dishes,
Greens on a white table.
Nimble fingers, raw foods —
Gaudy colors, mixed.

Water wells up in a glass —
Ready to quench the thirsty.
And a young girl on the lawn
Falls silent: day is passing away.

שטילקייט

רויטע מערן, שיסלען בלויען,
גרינסן אויף א ווײַסן טיש.
פֿלינקע פֿינגער, שפּײַזן רויע —
בונטע פֿארבן אין געמיש.

וואסער שפּרודלט אינעם גלאָז —
דורשטיקן צו שטילן גרייט.
און דאָס מיידעלע אין גראָז
שווײַגט: דער טאָג פֿארגייט.

So Many Warm Words

Mother's Death

The shadows arrived in silence.
Their steps crushed our happiness.
With long hands, they seized our mother —
Never to return.

The fever in her limbs had quieted.
Mother searched around her bed:
"Is there a candle?" — and said, as from the *Siddur*,
The final prayer of the dying.

The day still sang of summer,
Warmth streamed through the window glass,
And the prayer vanished from her lips —
Like dew on a withered flower.

דער מאַמעס טויט

די שטומע שאָטנס זײַנען אָנגעקומען,
צעטראָטן אונדזער גליק מיט טויבע טריט,
מיט לאַנגע הענט די מאַמע אָנגענומען —
מיט הענט, וואָסברענגען קיין מאָל ניט צוריק.

דער פיבער האָט געשטילט אין אירע גלידער.
די מאַמע האָט געזוכט אַרום איר בעט:
„האָסט ליכט?" — האָט זי געפרעגט, און ווי פון סידור,
געזאָגט דאָס לעצטע גוטסדיק גוטבעט.

דער טאָג האָט ווײַטער תּמוזדיק געזונגען,
די וואַרעמקייט געשטראָמט האָט דורך דער שויב,
און אויף איר מויל די תּפֿילה איז פאַרגאַנגען,
ווי אויף אַ וועלקנדיקער בלום — דער טוי.

So Many Warm Words

Like a Bee

The way a bee throws itself at a flower —
That's how I drink from your beauty, oh south.
By day the sun's rays gild me,
By night — the moon colors me blue.

I talk things through with the distant stars
That sparkle from heaven's tents.
How healing it is, to cry out my tears
In encounters with other worlds.

Rosa Nevadovska

ווי אַ בין

ווי אַ בין צו בלום צוגעפֿאַלן —
אַזוי טרינק איך פֿון דײַן שײנקייט, דרום.
בײַ טאָג מיך זוניקן די שטראַלן,
בײַ נאַכט — מיך בלוויִקט די לבֿנה.

איך רייד זיך דורך מיט די ווײַטע שטערן —
זײ בלישטשען פֿון די הימל-געצעלטן.
רפֿואהדיק וויין איך אוים מײַנע טרערן
אין באַגעגעניש מיט אַנדערע וועלטן.

*

In final tenderness, minutes diffuse like wonder,
Gentle hands extend like flowers through the dread.
In silence, a person sees her end and calmly gets ready
For blueness, distance and radiance.

Like snakes twisted together lie the unknown roads.
In silence a person calmly rests — prepared.
From everyone now parted, and everyone forgiven,
She merges with eternity — salt into bread.

אין צארטקייט לעצטער שפרייטן זיך, ווי ווונדער, די מינוטן
און אין די אננסטן צִיען זיך, ווי בלומען, לַיַכטע הענט.
אין שטילקייט זעט דער מענטש זיַן סוף, און גרייט זיך,
א בארוטער,
צו ווַיטקייט זיך אַוועקגעבן, צו בלויקייט און צו בלענד.

ווי אַיַנגעדרייטע שלאנגען ליגן אומבאקאנטע וועגן.
אין שטילקייט א בארוטער ליגט דער מענטש —
ער איז שוין גרייט.
פון אלעמען שוין אפגעשיידט, און אלעמען פארגעגעבן —
באהעפט זיך מיט דער אייביקייט, ווי זאָלץ מיט ליַב פון
ברויט.

So Many Warm Words   53

A Little Poem

In the oven, a hellish fire burns,
And wood weeps with tarry tears.
You are dear to me, my far-off friend —
Through the storm, your voice comes clear.

The bushes enrobed with snow
Bring me your soft greetings.
My gloom, my pain, my woe —
You will discover in this poem.

אַ לידעלע

אין אויוון ברענט העליש דאָס פֿײַער,
דאָס האָלץ וויינט מיט פּעכיקע טרערן.
מיַן פֿרײַנד אין דער וויַט, ביסט מיר טײַער —
דיַן שטים דורך די שנייען כ׳קאָן הערן.

די קוסטעם, פֿאַרטוליעט אין שנייען,
מיר ברענגען פֿון דיר שטילע גרוסן.
מיַן אומעט, מיַן פּיַן, מיַנע וויייען —
וועסט דו דורך מיַן ליד זיך דערוויסן.

War

The sun won't be back to the field.
Corn stalks have long turned to straw.
Autumn flowers have wilted.
The gray sky swells with tears.

Drops of rain unleash a rhythm;
It sounds like a sorrowful drum.
Mother wants to run out to meet him:
She thinks it's her son.

And the barn doors hang open,
And the fruit blushes to ripeness.
For a while, the wind has kept hidden.
In silence, a leaf falls to earth.

Rosa Nevadovska

מלחמה

צום פעלד וועט דער זון מער ניט קומען.
פון זאַנגען געוואָרן איז שטרוי.
עס וויאַנען שוין האַרבסטיקע בלומען.
דער הימל פאַרוויינט איז און גרוי.

עס פּיקלען די טראָפּנס פון רעגן
דעם ריטעם פון טרויער-געזאַנג.
די מאַמע וויל לויפן אַנטקעגן:
ס'איז אפשר דער זון מיט זײַן גאַנג?

און עפֿענע טירן פון שײַער,
און פֿרוכטן זיך רויטלען צו זאַט.
דער ווינט האָט אַ וויַיל זיך פאַרטיַיעט.
צו דר'ערד פאַלט אין שטילקייט אַ בלאַט.

At My Window

A gray cat, and beyond — green branches.
Quietly, the spring day is passing.
I love silence, the sound of deep stillness.
I love the gloom-light when the sun departs.

I love the thoughtfulness of tall trees;
I love the earth's warm depth.
I love being mastered by the dread
Of that voice, heard throughout the world.

בײַ מײַן פֿענצטער

אַ גרויע קאַץ, און איבער איר — די גרינע צווײַגן.
דער פֿרילינגדיקער טאָג אין שווײַגעניש פֿאַרגייט.
כ'האָב ליב די שטילקייטן, די שטים פֿון טיפֿן שווײַגן;
כ'האָב ליב דאָס אומעטליכט ווען זון מיט אונדז זיך שיידט.

כ'האָב ליב די טראַכטעניש פֿון הויכע קלוגע ביימער;
כ'האָב ליב די וואַרעמקייט, די טיפֿע, פֿון דער ערד;
כ'האָב ליב באַהערשט צו ווערן פֿון דער אימה
פֿאַר יענעם קול, וואָס דורך דער וועלט זיך הערט.

So Many Warm Words

Tree in a Field

A naked tree stands alone in a field,
Its brown bark scraped and gashed.
Rude winter stole the last leaf hanging,
Carried it off to its lair.

No fellow tree, no roof, no village.
Last night's snow extinguished the stars,
and its horrible whirlwind drowned out
All voices. Now, just silence.

The gaunt tree waits patiently
For the murmur of flowering forests;
The loner — stubbornly persisting
To become just one spring older.

Rosa Nevadovska

אַ בוים אין פעלד

אַ בוים אַ נאַקעטער אין פעלד אַליין,
צערונצלט און צעקאַרבט זייַן ברוינע קאָרע.
דאָס לעצטע בלעטעלע דער ווינטער האָט גענומען
פֿון אים געהרויבט, פֿאַרטראָגן אין אַ נאָרע.

קיין ברודער-בוים, קיין ייִשוב און קיין דאַך.
דער שנײ האָט אויסגעלאָשן אַלע שטערן.
דער ווירבלווינט פֿון שוידערלעכער נאַכט
פֿאַרטרונקען האָט די קולות — נישט צום הערן.

דער אויסגעדאַרטער בוים געדולדיק וואַרט
אויף דעם גערויש פֿון בליִענדיקע וועלדער;
דער איינזאַמער — ער האָט זיך איינגעשפּאַרט
צו ווערן קאַטש מיט נאָך אַ פרילינג עלטער.

So Many Warm Words

Butterflies

In the room, illuminated lamps
Peer into the night like golden eyes.
From marsh and forests, drawn toward the light
Come airy butterflies.

They flutter around the fire's glow —
Seeking day and sunny warmth.
The light delivers them, for now
From darkness, damp and swamp.

Butterflies, so blithe and easy,
They dance in a rainbow chain of breath.
I watch, clenching my fingers —
The slightest touch could bring them death.

שמעטערלינגען

אין צימער האָבן אויפֿגעהעלט די לאָמפּן,
ווי אויגן גאָלדענע, באַקוקט די נאַכט.
דאָס ליכט האָט פֿון די וועלדער און די זומפּן
שמעטערלינגען לופֿטיקע געבראַכט.

זיי פֿלאַטערן אַרום דער שײַן פֿון פֿײַער —
זיי זוכן וואַרעמקייט און טאָגיקייט און זון.
זיי מיינען, אַז דאָס ליכט איז אַ באַפֿרײַער
פֿון פֿינצטערניש, פֿון נאַסקייט, פֿון דער זומפּ.

שמעטערלינגען לופֿטיקע און גרינגע
זיי טאַנצן אין אַ רעגנבויגן־קייט.
איך קוק — און האַלט פֿאַרקלעמט מײַנע פֿינגער —
אַ יעדער ריר קאָן ברענגען איצט דעם טויט.

So Many Warm Words

A Mountain of Pain

Words live, as real as day,
They breathe with the same breath;
They rejoice quietly and share my lament.
My suffering rests in a poem, like light in its shadow.

A mountain of pain presses into the lines of my poem —
And years of living and striving.
My words, illuminated by fire —
Blue veins weave among them.

אַ באַרג פֿײַן

עס לעבן די װערטער, װי װאַר פֿון דעם טאָג,
זײ אָטעמען מיט'ן זעלביקן אָטעם;
זײ פֿרײען־זיך שטיל און קלאָגן מײַן קלאָג —
מײַן פּײַן רוט אין ליד, װי ליכט אין זײַן שאָטן...

אַ באַרג פֿון פּײַן שטראָמט־אַרײַן אין די שורות פֿון ליד —
און יאָרן פֿון לעבן און שטאַרעבן...
העלד'אױף אין די װערטער פֿײַער און ליכט,
און אָדערן בלױע זיך־װעבן.

Snow

Snow on trees, snow on houses.
Blinding white. Skies gray and torn.
In my mind's eye, I am traveling
To my city that is no more.

Deep silences are spreading there.
Not a single voice is heard.
A solitary crow steals over fields,
Blackens unsown earth.

Graves. —The millions lie,
Buried or left where they fell.
Amid the ashes, winds are howling
One song to cradle all.

Rosa Nevadovska

שניי

שניי אויף ביימער, שניי אויף שטיבער.
ווײַסער בלענד. די הימלען גרא.
איצטער טראָג איך זיך אַריבער
צו מײַן שטאָט, וואָס איז ניטאָ.

טיפע שטילקייטן זיך שפּרייטן
און קיין קול פון דאָרט ניטאָ.
איבער פעלדער ניט-פאַרזייטע
שוואַרצט אַ שנאָבלדיקע קראָ.

קברים. די מיליאָנען ליגן —
ווער באַהאַלטן און ווער ניט.
ווינטן וואיען און פאַרוויגן
אַלע אַשן מיט איין ליד.

On the Final Road
(for little Leah)

The Moscow night — bitter cold.
Frost, sleepless, stood guard.
Watched over streets and houses,
Ushered in glittering snow.

Through Moscow's snowy expanse,
On a drifted boulevard, in pain,
A mother bent into the wind
With her child — on the final road.

אין לעצטן גאַנג

(לאהי'לעז)

קאַלט איז די מאָסקװוער נאַכט.
דער פֿראָסט ניט געשלאָפֿן, געװאַכט.
הײַזער און גאַסן באַװאַכט
בריליאַנטענע שנייען געבראַכט.

איבער'ן ברייטן מאָסקװוער שניי,
אין װײַ אויף פֿאַרשנייטן שאָסײַ —
געגאַנגען איז מאַמע אין װינט
דעם לעצטן גאַנג מיט איר קינד.

Pay Attention

Pay attention to the quiet.
Don't you detect it? Do you hear?
The dumbness, the silence of stone and of star.

Surely — can't you hear it?
The muteness, silence at the ends of the earth.
Blood's being spilled there —
Ceaselessly it will pour forth.

April 17th 1944

הער זיך איַן

הער זיך איַן אין דער שטילקייט.
דו הערסט? וואָס קאָנסטו דערהערן?
די שטומקייט, די שטילקייט פון שטיין און פון שטערן.

וואָס קאָנסטו דערהערן?
די שטומקייט, די שטילקייט פון יענער זיַט ערד.
דאָס בלוט ווערט פאַרגאָסן,
כּסדר פאַרגאָסן עס ווערט.

17טן אַפּריל 1944

For Darling Leah
November 13th, 1915

Pale face, gray eyes,
Luminous fair hair.
A deep sorrow veiled
Your scant two years.

From the blue fields of home
Through Ukrainian steppes,
To the green Moscow woods —
This was your short road.

With eyes wide in wonder,
You soaked up the world
Turning toward warmth, in fear —
Before the final cold.

Rosa Nevadovska

ליעטשקען

13טן נאָוועמבער 1915

בלאַסער פּנים, גרויע אויגן.
העלע, לײַכטע, ליבע האָר.
טיפֿער טרויער האָט פֿאַרצויגן
דײַנע קורצינקע צוויי יאָר.

פֿון די היימיש־בלויע פֿעלדער,
דורך אוקראַיִנישן סטעפּ —
צו די גרינע מאַסקווער וועלדער
איז געווען דײַן קורצער וועג.

מיט פֿאַרוווּנדערט־גרויסע אויגן
האָסטו אײַנגעזאַפּט די וועלט.
זיך צו וואַרעמקייט געצויגן
אין דער שרעק פֿאַר לעצטער קעלט.

So Many Warm Words

Going to Sleep

Mama, must I go to sleep now?
Is it really night again?
Did the day run away?
Or did someone make it die?

Yes, the stars are winking now,
Behind me, in the far-off sky.
Mama, soon enough I'll learn
How time flees, it flies.

Mama, will you sing again
A lullaby to help me sleep?
Silvery bells will tinkle, follow
After shepherd with his sheep.

Again I'll count the stars, until
I barely am awake to see
And after that I'll fall asleep
For a long night.

And after that I'll fall asleep
For a long night.

Rosa Nevadovska

שלאָפֿן־גיין

מאַמע, מוז איך גיין שוין שלאָפֿן?
איז שוין טאַקע ווידער נאַכט?
ווּ זשע איז דער טאָג אַנטלאָפֿן?
צי מען האָט אים אומגעבראַכט?

יאָ, עס צינדן זיך די שטערן
הינטער מיר, אין הימל, ווײַט.
מאַמע, באַלד וועל איך דערהערן,
ווי עס פֿליט, פֿאַרפֿליט די צײַט.

מאַמע, וועסטו ווידער זינגען
מיר דאָס ליד פֿון קינדער־שלאָף?
זילבער־גלעקלעך וועלן קלינגען
נאָכן פֿאַסטעך מיט די שאָף.

איך וועל ווידער ציילן שטערן,
ביז איך וועל נאָר זײַן נאָך וואַך
און דערנאָך אַנטשלאָפֿן ווערן
אויף אַ לאַנגער נאַכט.

און דערנאָך אַנטשלאָפֿן ווערן
אויף אַ לאַנגער נאַכט.

So Many Warm Words

Mother and Child

In the spaces of late dusk
The Jewish mother of fire

Edged in gray ash
Turns toward her dear son.

Her little one drifts on high
And yearns to get close to his mother.
In clouds and smoke, they both
Still burn in extinguished skies.

מאַמע און קינד

אין שפּעטע פֿאַרנאַכטיקע רוימען
די ייִדישע מאַמע פֿון פֿײַער
אין גרויע פֿאַראַשיקטע זוימען —
ציט זיך צו איר זונעלע טײַערס.

איר זונעלע שווימט אין די הייכן
און וויל צו דער מאַמען גענענען.
זיי ביידע — אין וואָלקנס און רויכן —
אין פֿאַרלאָשענע הימלען נאָך ברענען.

So Many Warm Words

Fire-Script
In memory of my closest ones, in Treblinka

The darkness rushed along, carrying untamed
A torn-out page, a sheet of monstrous flame.

The paper bore no letters, empty of any writ
Yet a deeper, greater meaning still clung to it.

The page flew up so high, the clouds became its kin
And its incandescence split the darkness open.

Who is snapping red, catching in a breeze?
A bit of night-fire from Treblinka's chimneys?

Perhaps a Torah parchment? Or a scroll in flame?
Fragment of a record of exterminated names?

The paper flickers to a cloud, ignites it and flies higher —
Leaving ashes in its wake, the remnants of a pyre.

Sounds begin to stir, a voice ascends and speaks —
Through darkened territories, over cities, seas:

"This page will be preserved, sealed and kept secret —
With it I'll punish nations, as with the ancient tablets.

"A reckoning for bodies burnt and sacred books unsaved —
I will demand my due for all, for every brother's grave.

"And for the ones incinerated, cut down without a trace,
I will keep this writ of fire until the end of days."

The page was extinguished, consumed entirely by flame.
Only tongues of fire-speech remained.

Rosa Nevadovska

פײַער־כתב

מײַנע נאָענטסטע אין טרעבלינקע — לזכרון

דער חושך האָט געטראָגן מיט שנעלקײט אומגעהײַער
אן אָפּגעריסן בלאַט, אַ בלאַט פֿון פֿלאַקער־פֿײַער.

דאָס בלאַט האָט ניט קײן אותיות, גאָרנישט אױפֿגעשריבן,
נאָר טיפֿער, גרױסער זינען איז אױף אים פֿאַרבליבן.

דאָס בלאַט פֿליט אין דער הײך, ברידערט זיך מיט װאָלקנס,
זײַן גליִענדיקער רױט האָט דעם חושך אױפֿגעשפּאַלטן.

— װער איז דאָס רױטע בלאַט, װאָס פֿליט אין הױכע רױמען?
אַ שטיק פֿײַער אין דער נאַכט, פֿון טרעבלינקער קױמען?

אַ תּורה־פֿאַרמעט אפֿשר? צי פֿלאַמען פֿון מגילות?
אַ טײל פֿון די פּנקסים פֿון פֿאַרטיליקטע קהילות?

דאָס בלאַט פֿליט אױף אַ װאָלקן, צינדט אים אָן און פֿליט װײַטער,
לאָזט איבער נאָך זיך אַשן, שיריים פֿונעם שײַטער.

אַ קול הײבט אָן זיך װעקן, די שטים שטײַגט הױך און רעדט —
דורך חושך, דורך שטחים, איבער ימים, שטעט:

„דאָס בלאַט װערט אָפּגעהיט, פֿאַרזיגלט און באַהאַלטן —
מיט אים כ׳װעל פֿעלקער שטראָפֿן, װי מיט די לוחות אַלטע.

„אַ חשבון איז דאָס פֿאַר פֿאַרברענטע גופֿים, ספֿרים,
און מאַנען כ׳װעל פֿאַר אַליץ, פֿאַר אַלע ברידער־קבֿרים,

„און אױך פֿאַר די, װאָס מ׳האָט אָן שפּור פֿאַרברענט,
פֿאַרשניטן —
װעל איך דאָס כּתבֿ פֿון פֿײַער אין אײביקײט פֿאַרהיטן."—

דאָס בלאַט האָט דורכגעפֿלאַקערט און זיך אױסגעלאָשן,
נאָר געבליבן איז די שטים פֿון פֿײַער־לשון.

So Many Warm Words

A Vision

The mountains will crumble, the sea will engulf them,
Chaos will cover the earth.
The world will sink into rings of water, and from
The abyss — not a sound will be heard.

And over the waters the moon will rise,
Never witnessed again by a human eye.
The seas will churn, mumble stories of danger,
and of the earth, which once was a flower.

But somewhere, far-off, poems will drift —
the surviving yearning and words of a poet.
Over the wastes and beneath the great chasms
our plea will be sung into the infinite.

אַ זעונג

די בערג וועלן צעפֿאַלן, דער ים וועט זיי פֿאַרשלינגען,
אַ תּוהו ובוהו וועט זײַן אויף דער ערד.
די וועלט וועט פֿאַרזינקען אין וואַסער־רינגען
אַראָפּ אין די תּהומען — פֿון קיינעם ניט דערהערט.

און איבער די וואַסערן וועט אויפֿגיין די לבנה.
קיין מענטשנס אויג וועט איר פּנים מער ניט זען.
די ימים וועלן מורמלען, דערציילן פֿון סכנות,
פֿון דער ערד, וואָס איז אַ מאָל אַ בלום געווען.

נאָר ערגעץ, אין ווײַט, וועלן טראָגן זיך לידער —
פֿאַרבליבענע בענקשאַפֿט און וואַרט פֿון פּאָעט,
און איבער דער וויסטקייט — אין תּהום און אין נידער —
צו אייביקייט זינגען וועט אונדזער געבעט.

So Many Warm Words

*

I would flay off my own skin,
Undo the burden of flesh and bones.
Let me be held together with rays of light
So I can befriend the winds of the world,
Be done with my body and shine
Easily as the mid-month night —
Beaming into the darkness.

✡

איך וואָלט פֿון זיך אַליין די הויט געשונדן.
אַ לאַסט איז מיר דאָס לײַב אויף מײַנע ביינער.
מיט שטילע שטראַלן וויל איך זײַן פֿאַרבונדן,
זיך חברן מיט ווינטן פֿון דער וועלט,
און זײַן אויס גוף, און ווערן לײַכט און העל,
ווי נאַקעט אין מיטן חודש —
און לײַכטן אין דעם חושך.

At the Shore

I stand by the sea, watch it struggle and strain,
I hear the voice rumble from its abyss,
And it seems I am myself transformed
Into a drop of sea-water, a wave.

Now I rise up on the waters, now I fall into the depths,
Now I am born, then disappear,
Battered against the sharp stones of reefs…
I am no more…. and again I take form.

אויפן ברעג

איך שטיי ביַי דעם ים, איך זע זיַין געראַנגל,
איך הער פון זיַין אפגרונט די שטים,
און ס'דוכט זיך מיר אויס: איך אַליין וועד פאַרוואַנדלט
אין זיַין וועל, אין אַ טראָפּן פון אים.

אָט שטײַג איך אויף כוואַליעס, אָט פאַל איך אין טיפן,
אָט וועד איך געבוירן, פאַרשוווּנדן איך וועד,
צעשלאָג זיך אָן שפּיציקע שטיינער פון ריפן —
אָט בין איך ניטאָ מער... און ווידער איך וועד.

So Many Warm Words

Yearning

How quiet it is! I need no one today.
Mountains surround me — rising to highest heaven.
I am a friend of mountains now, and distance,
And a wisp of silver connects us.

High up drifts an eagle, freely —
Take me, eagle, on your far-off journey!
From there, I'll glimpse the world anew —
Taking on a bird's view.

And maybe — I'll become an eagle, too,
Soaring higher, to see the sun's heart.
My veins will run dark with wine
And from my back, wings will part.

בענקשאַפט

ווי שטיל דאָ איז! איך דאַרף ניט קיינעם היַינט.
אַרום מיר בערג — זיי שטייַגן העכער הימל.
פֿון באַרג און וויַיטשקייט בין איך איצט אַ פֿריַינד,
און צווישן זיי און מיר — אַ זילבערדרימל.

אַן אָדלער טראָגט זיך אין די הייכן פֿריַי.
נעם מיך, אָדלער, אין דיַין וועג דעם וויַיטן!
פֿון דאָרט וועל איך די וועלט דערזען אויף ס'ניַי —
און אפֿשר אויף אַ פֿויגל זיך פֿאַרביַיטן.

און אפֿשר — אפֿשר אויך אַן אָדלער זיַין,
זיך טראָגן העכער, דאָס האַרץ פֿון זון באַקוקן.
מיַין בלוט וועט ווערן טונקל-רויטער וויַין —
און פֿליגל וועלן וואַקסן אויף מיַין רוקן.

So Many Warm Words

Morning-joy

Silent streams of light saturate me:
I become transparent, like amber.
Who am I now? — A world from somewhere
Gliding sanely through eternity.

I come to the sea's edge. Shore and water
Are all I see, in a world made pure.
Who am I now? A grain of sand, some dust
That drifts into the future even further.

I face the mountains. My gaze fills with light.
I stand erect. I wait for something great.
I myself become a mountain, my countenance — petrified.
And my fingertips write these very letters.

מאָרגנפרייד

די שטילע שטראַמען ליכט מיך דרינגען דורך,
און איך װער דורכזיכטיק, װי די בורשטינען.
װער בין איך איצט? אַ װעלט פון ערגעץ־װוּ
שטראַמט דורך דער אייביקייט ביַים פולן זינען.

איך קום צים ברעג פון ים. װערט פול מיַין אויג
מיט ברעג און װאַסער און דעם װעלט־געליַיטער.
װער בין איך איצט? אַ זעמדעלע, אַ שטויב,
װאָס טראָגט זיך אין דעם מאָרגן ערגעץ װיַיטער.

מיַין פנים — צו די בערג. מיַין בליק װערט פול מיט ליכט.
איך גליַיך זיך אויס. איך װאַרט אויף עפעס גרויסעם.
איך װער אַליין אַ באַרג, פאַרשטיינערט — מיַין געזיכט,
און פינגערשפיצן מיַינע שריַיבן אָט די אותיות.

Desert

How dazzling and endless you are:
Despite all storms, you hold your peace.
My intimate, faithful desert
I see you in all things, everywhere.

In cities such as ours, in stone,
In all the walls of skyscrapers,
In me, so singular, alone —
Your desolation burns.

But we lack your fiery speech,
Your outcries and sharp silences.
Locked deep within us you rest,
The way our pain does — in muteness.

Rosa Nevadovska

מדבר

ווי בלענדנדיק און ענדלאָז ביסטו,
מיט אַלע שטורעמס ביסטו שטום.
מײַן נאָענטע און טרײַע וויסטע,
אין אַלץ איך זע דיך, אומעטום.

אין שטעט, אין אונדזערע, אויף שטיינער,
אין אַלע הויכע מויערוואָנט,
אין מיר, דער איינזאַמער, דער איינער —
דײַן עלנט מדברדיקער ברענט.

נאָר ס׳פֿעלט אונדז אויס דײַן בליציק לשון,
דײַן שווײַגן און דײַן אויסגעשרײַ,
און טיף אין אונדז דו ליגסט פֿאַרשלאָסן,
ווי ס׳ליגט אין שטומקייט אונדזער ווײ.

So Many Warm Words

Seen

I have seen
your sunset in southern flames
when the minutes tumble down;
The brightness becomes monstrous
and afterwards —
devoured by hard shadows.

Only
your death
kindles within me a shining sorrow
that purifies
without cease.

געזען

איך האָב געזען
דײַן זונפֿאַרגאַנג אין דרום-פֿלאַקער,
ווען ס'פֿאַלן די רגעם אַראָפּ;
די ליכטיקייט ווערט אומגעהויער
און דערנאָך —
אין שווערע שאָטנם פֿאַרשלונגען.

נאָר
פֿון דײַן פֿאַרגאַנג
לײַכט טרויער-ליכטיקייט אין מיר
און לײַטערט
אָן אַן אויפֿהער.

Sea

Pearl. Gold. Silvery sky.
Wave-sway. Longing and poetry.
Enchanted song. Sleepy lull.
Sea, take me with you!

Take me, carry me to other lands.
I'll be your melody and like you, I'll sing.
In the sun's luster, I'll dazzle and shimmer,
In endless unrest, sing of peace.

Sky and distance. Misty colors.
Within me, silence — and a voice that glows.
All will be well with me, to be, until dying —
A grain of sand on the world's shore.

ים

פּערל. גאָלד. זילבער אין הימל.
וועלן-געוויג. בענקשאַפֿט און ליד.
צויבער-געזאַנג. געוויג ווי אין דרימל.
ים, נעם מיך מיט!

נעם מיך און טראָג מיך צו לאַנד און צו לענדער.
איך וויל זײַן דײַן ניגון און זינגען, ווי דו.
אין שימער פֿון זון וועל איך לײַכטן און בלענדן,
אין אייביקן אומרו זינגען פֿון רו.

הימל און ווײַטקייט. נעפּליקע פֿאַרבן.
שטילקייט אין מיר — און אַ שטים אויפֿגעהעלט.
באַלד וועט מיר גוט זײַן ביז אויסגיין, ביז שטאַרבן —
אַ זעמדעלע זײַן אויף דער וועלט.

Obedient

I comprehend the sand's voice,
Grasp what the stone says.
I listen to the hymns of rivers,
And the lament in a drop of water.

And I myself
Am sand and dust
Between earth and stars.
I send praise to God, blessed-be-He.
He will hear me.

הָאַרְכִיק

איך פארנעם פון זאמד די שטים,
איך פארנעם דאָס קול פון שטיין,
איך הער פון טײַכן דעם הימן,
איך הער פון טראָפּן דאָס געוויין.

און איך אליין —
בין זאמד און שטויב
צווישן ערד און שטערן.
איך שיק גאָט ברוך הוא א לויב.
ער וועט מיך דערהערן.

I Have Seen

I have seen the radiant dazzle
Of the hour before the stars ascend.
I have seen, at the height of day, its end —
And thought about beginnings that vanish.

I have stood astonished: around me
Heavenly bodies shimmered and dimmed,
And a wind, with a light touch
Spoke to the world in a gesture of silence.

Rosa Nevadovska

איך האָב געזען

איך האָב געזען דעם שטראַליקן געבלענד
אין דער שעה פֿאַרן אויפֿשטײַג פֿון שטערן;
איך האָב געזען פֿון הויכן טאָג דעם ענד —
איך האָב געטראַכט פֿון אויפֿקום און ניט־ווערן.

איך בין געשטאַנען אין פֿאַרגאַף: אַרום מיר
האָבן ליכטער זיך געמיניעט און געלאָשן,
און אַ ווינט האָט מיט לײַכטן באַריר
צו דער וועלט גערעדט מיט שטום־לשון.

About the Author

Yiddish poet Rosa Nevadovska (1890–1971), grew up in Bialystok when it was a part of Russia. She studied in Eastern and Central Europe, returned to her native city after World War I and ultimately immigrated to the United States in 1928. As a writer and journalist in this country, she traveled, lecturing, writing and residing in various cities, from New York City to Venice, California. Nevadovska published just one volume of poems in her lifetime, *Azoy vi ikh bin* (As I Am; 1936). However, she wrote many more poems which never appeared in the Yiddish newspapers or journals of her day. It was her request to her family that they be published upon her death. These moving poems were collected in the anthology, *Lider mayne* (My Poetry), which came out in 1974.

About the Translator

Poet Merle Lyn Bachman fell in love with Rosa Nevadovska's poems when she was in graduate school in her hometown of Albany, New York and first writing her book *Recovering Yiddishland: Threshold Moments in American Literature* (2009). In 2015-16, Bachman was granted a Translation Fellowship at the Yiddish Book Center, where she worked on the draft of this very book, *So Many Warm Words*. Bachman, a former denizen of Oakland, California and Louisville, Kentucky, now resides, writes and translates in Bloomington, Indiana.
See https://www.merlebachman.com/ for more.

The Jewish Poetry Project

jpoetry.us

Ben Yehuda Press

From the Coffee House of Jewish Dreamers: Poems of Wonder and Wandering and the Weekly Torah Portion by Isidore Century

"Isidore Century is a wonderful poet. His poems are funny, deeply observed, without pretension." – *The Jewish Week*

The House at the Center of the World: Poetic Midrash on Sacred Space by Abe Mezrich

"Direct and accessible, Mezrich's midrashic poems often tease profound meaning out of his chosen Torah texts. These poems remind us that our Creator is forgiving, that the spiritual and physical can inform one another, and that the supernatural can be carried into the everyday."
—Yehoshua November, author of *God's Optimism*

**we who desire:
Poems and Torah riffs by Sue Swartz**

"Sue Swartz does magnificent acrobatics with the Torah. She takes the English that's become staid and boring, and adds something that's new and strange and exciting. These are poems that leave a taste in your mouth, and you walk away from them thinking, what did I just read? Oh, yeah. It's the Bible."
—Matthue Roth, author of *Yom Kippur A Go-Go*

Open My Lips: Prayers and Poems by Rachel Barenblat

"Barenblat's God is a personal God—one who lets her cry on His shoulder, and who rocks her like a colicky baby. These poems bridge the gap between the ineffable and the human. This collection will bring comfort to those with a religion of their own, as well as those seeking a relationship with some kind of higher power."
—Satya Robyn, author of *The Most Beautiful Thing*

Words for Blessing the World: Poems in Hebrew and English by Herbert J. Levine

"These writings express a profoundly earth-based theology in a language that is clear and comprehensible. These are works to study and learn from."
—Rodger Kamenetz, author of *The Jew in the Lotus*

Shiva Moon: Poems by Maxine Silverman

"The poems, deeply felt, are spare, spoken in a quiet but compelling voice, as if we were listening in to her inner life. This book is a precious record of the transformation saying Kaddish can bring."
—Howard Schwartz, author of *The Library of Dreams*

is: heretical Jewish blessings and poems by Yaakov Moshe (Jay Michaelson)

"Finally, Torah that speaks to and through the lives we are actually living: expanding the tent of holiness to embrace what has been cast out, elevating what has been kept down, advancing what has been held back, reveling in questions, revealing contradictions."
—Eden Pearlstein, aka eprhyme

Texts to the Holy: Poems
by Rachel Barenblat

"These poems are remarkable, radiating a love of God that is full bodied, innocent, raw, pulsating, hot, drunk. I can hardly fathom their faith but am grateful for the vistas they open. I will sit with them, and invite you to do the same."
—Merle Feld, author of *A Spiritual Life*

The Sabbath Bee: Love Songs to Shabbat
by Wilhelmina Gottschalk

"Torah, say our sages, has seventy faces. As these prose poems reveal, so too does Shabbat. Here we meet Shabbat as familiar housemate, as the child whose presence transforms a family, as a spreading tree, as an annoying friend who insists on being celebrated, as a woman, as a man, as a bee, as the ocean."
—Rachel Barenblat, author of *The Velveteen Rabbi's Haggadah*

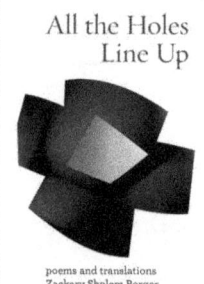

All the Holes Line Up: Poems and Translations
by Zackary Sholem Berger

"Spare and precise, Berger's poems gaze unflinchingly at—but also celebrate—human imperfection in its many forms. And what a delight that Berger also includes in this collection a handful of his resonant translations of some of the great Yiddish poets." —Yehoshua November, author of *God's Optimism* and *Two World Exist*

How to Bless the New Moon:
Songs of the Sovereign and the Icon
by Rachel Kann

"Rachel Kann is a master wordsmith. Her poems are rich in content, packed with life's wisdom and imbued with soul. May this collection of her work enable more of the world to enjoy her offerings."
—Sarah Yehudit Schneider, author of *You Are What You Hate* and *Kabbalistic Writings on the Nature of Masculine and Feminine*

Into My Garden
by David Caplan

"The beauty of Caplan's book is that it is not polemical. It does not set out to win an argument or ask you whether you've put your tefillin on today. These gentle poems invite the reader into one person's profound, ambiguous religious experience."
—*The Jewish Review of Books*

Between the Mountain and the Land is the Lesson: Poetic Midrash on Sacred Community
by Abe Mezrich

"Abe Mezrich cuts straight back to the roots of the Midrashic tradition, sermonizing as a poet, rather than ideologue. Best of all, Abe knows how to ask questions and avoid the obvious answers."
—Jake Marmer, author of *Jazz Talmud*

NOKADDISH: Poems in the Void
by Hanoch Guy Kaner

"A subversive, midrashic play with meanings—specifically Jewish meanings, and then the reversal and negation of these meanings."
—Robert G. Margolis

An Added Soul: Poems for a New Old Religion
by Herbert J. Levine

"These poems are remarkable, radiating a love of God that is full bodied, innocent, raw, pulsating, hot, drunk. I can hardly fathom their faith but am grateful for the vistas they open. I will sit with them, and invite you to do the same."
—Merle Feld, author of *A Spiritual Life.*

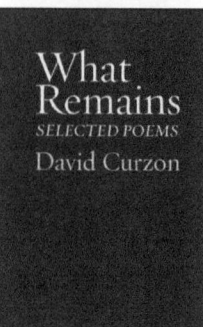

What Remains
by David Curzon

"Aphoristic, ekphrastic, and precise revelations animate WHAT REMAINS. In his stunning rewriting of Psalm 1 and other biblical passages, Curzon shows himself to be a fabricator, a collector, and an heir to the literature, arts, and wisdom traditions of the planet."
—Alicia Ostriker, author of *The Volcano and After*

The Shortest Skirt in Shul
by Sass Oron

"These poems exuberantly explore gender, Torah, the masks we wear, and the way our bodies (and the ways we wear them) at once threaten stable narratives, and offer the kind of liberation that saves our lives."
—Alicia Jo Rabins, author of *Divinity School*, composer of *Girls In Trouble*

Walking Triptychs
by Ilya Gutner

These are poems from when I walked about Shanghai and thought about the meaning of the Holocaust.

Book of Failed Salvation
by Julia Knobloch

"These beautiful poems express a tender longing for spiritual, physical, and emotional connection. They detail a life in movement—across distances, faith, love, and doubt."
—David Caplan, author of *Into My Garden*

Daily Blessings: Poems on Tractate Berakhot
by Hillel Broder

"Hillel Broder does not just write poetry about the Talmud; he also draws out the Talmud's poetry, finding lyricism amidst legality and re-setting the Talmud's rich images like precious gems in end-stopped lines of verse."
—Ilana Kurshan, author of *If All the Seas Were Ink*

The Missing Jew: Poems 1976-2022
by Rodger Kamenetz

"How does Rodger Kamenetz manage to have so singular a voice and at the same time precisely encapsulate the world view of an entire generation (also mine) of text-hungry American Jews born in the middle of the twentieth century?"
—Jacqueline Osherow, author of *Ultimatum from Paradise* and *My Lookalike at the Krishna Temple: Poems*

The Red Door: A dark fairy tale told in poems
by Shawn C. Harris

"THE RED DOOR, like its poet author Shawn C. Harris, transcends genres and identities. It is an exploration in crossing worlds. It brings together poetry and story telling, imagery and life events, spirit and body, the real and the fantastic, Jewish past and Jewish present, to spin one tale."
—Einat Wilf, author of *The War of Return*

The Matter of Families
by Robert H. Deluty

"Robert Deluty's career-spanning collection of New and Selected poems captures the essence of his work: the power of love, joy, and connection, all tied together with the poet's glorious sense of humor. This book is Deluty's masterpiece."
—Richard M. Berlin, M.D., author of *Freud on My Couch*

The Five Books of Limericks
by Rhonda Rosenheck

"A biblical commentary that is truly unique. Each chapter of the Torah is distilled into its own limerick, leading the reader to reconsider the meaning of the original text, and opening avenues for interpretation that are both fun and insightful."
—Rabbi Hillel Norry

Bits and Pieces
by Edward Pomerantz

"A stunning tapestry of family life in the 40s and 50s. Like all great poetry, Pomerantz's work expands after reading. Each poem is exquisitely structured, often with a stunning ending, into a masterful whole."
—Alan Ziegler, editor of SHORT: *An International Anthology*

Words for a Dazzling Firmament: Poems/Readings on Bereishit Through Shemot
by Abe Mezrich

"Mezrich is a cultivated craftsman— interpretively astute, sonically deliberate, and spiritually cunning."
—Zohar Atkins, author of *Nineveh*

Everything Thaws
by R. B. Lemberg

"Full of glacier-sharp truths, and moments revealed between words like bodies beneath melting permafrost. As it becomes increasingly plain how deeply our world is shaped by war and climate change and grief and anger, articulating that shape feels urgent and necessary and painful and healing."
—Ruthanna Emrys, author of *A Half-Built Garden*

Ode to the Dove
An illustrated, bilingual edition of a Yiddish poem by Abraham Sutzkever
Zackary Sholem Berger, translator
Liora Ostroff, Illustrator

"An elegant volume for lovers of poetry."
—Justin Cammy, translator of *Sutzkever, From the Vilna Ghetto to Nuremberg: Memoir and Testimony*

Poems for a Cartoon Mouse
by Andrew Burt

"Andrew Burt's poetry magnifies the vanishingly small line between danger and safety. This collection asks whether order is an illusion that veils chaos, or vice-versa, juxtaposing images from the Bible with animated films."
—Ari Shapiro, host of NPR's *All Things Considered*

Old Shul
by Pinny Bulman

"Nostalgia gives way to a tender theology, a softly chuckling illumination from within the heart of/as a beautiful, broken sanctuary, somehow both gritty and fragile, grimy and iridescent – not unlike faith itself."
—Jake Marmer, author of *Cosmic Diaspora*

Feet In L.A., But My Womb Lives In Jerusalem, My Breath In Vermont
by Lori Levy

"Reading through Lori Levy's new book of poems takes my breath away. With no pretense whatsoever, they leap, alive, from the page until this reader felt as if she were living Levy's life. How does the author do it?"
—Mary Jo Balistreri, author of *Still*

www.ingramcontent.com/pod-product-compliance
Lightning Source LLC
LaVergne TN
LVHW041339080426
835512LV00006B/532